Saving Water!

Jill McDougall

Contents

Water

People often talk about saving water. "What's all the fuss about?" you might ask.

Water may not seem very important – we just turn on a tap and... *whoosh*... out it comes!

Actually, there are many good reasons why we should care about saving water.

Whoosh!

Water is the most precious thing on Earth. Without water, nothing would **survive** – no plants, no animals and no people.

Water Use

We use water every day. We use it to take a shower, brush our teeth, wash the dishes and water the plants. Most importantly though, we drink it – and so does the dog!

Let's find out how much you know about using water.

Question:

Which of these activities use water?

- running a dairy farm
- cooking pasta
- putting out a fire

Answer:

All of them, of course!

Did You Know?

A dairy cow must drink about 11 litres of water to make three litres of milk!

Did you know that water is also used to make many of the things we buy?

Water is used to make the food we eat. It takes 2400 litres of water to make just one hamburger. That's more water than you could drink in a year!

We also use water to make our clothes. It takes 2700 litres of water to make a cotton T-shirt. That's the same as flushing your toilet 250 times!

A World of Water

The Earth looks blue from space. This is because most of the Earth's surface is covered in water. So, there must be plenty of water on Earth to go around... right?

This photo shows Earth as seen from space.

Hmmm, I wonder why they call it "Earth"? It should be called "Water"!

The truth is that we can't easily use a lot of the Earth's water. This is because most of it is found in the ocean as salt water.

Living things need fresh water, not salt water, to survive. Fresh water is water with little or no salt in it.

So where on Earth is all the fresh water?

Did You Know?

A person can live for around one month without food, but only a few days without fresh water!

In Search of Fresh Water

Antarctica is in the **Southern Hemisphere**. It is one of the coldest places on Earth. There is a lot of fresh water in Antarctica but it is frozen – so, it's ice!

In fact, most of the fresh water on Earth is frozen so it can't easily be used. Imagine towing an iceberg home to make a cool drink!

It's not nice being caught in the rain without an umbrella, but rain is a good thing. It's another **source** of the Earth's fresh water.

After it rains, the rainwater can end up in different places.

- Some rain falls into rivers, lakes and **reservoirs**.
- Some rain falls onto roofs and is stored in rainwater tanks.
- Some rain falls onto the ground and is soaked up.

Rain is falling into this reservoir.

Only a small amount of the fresh water that falls as rain can be used by people. This is because:

- Rain often falls over the ocean and mixes with seawater.
- Rain often falls over rivers. Some rivers flow to the ocean and mix with seawater, too.
- Rain is used by the Earth's trees and plants. They need it to survive.

This river flows into the ocean.

The Water Cycle

Have you ever wondered where rain comes from? Rain is actually water that has been used on Earth over and over again. We call this **process** the water cycle.

Here's how it works:

- When the air is warm, **water vapour** rises up from the ocean and forms clouds. Plants also lose water from their leaves.
- The clouds move across the land.
- Rain falls from the clouds.
- After falling to Earth, some rainwater flows back into the ocean.
- The water cycle starts again.

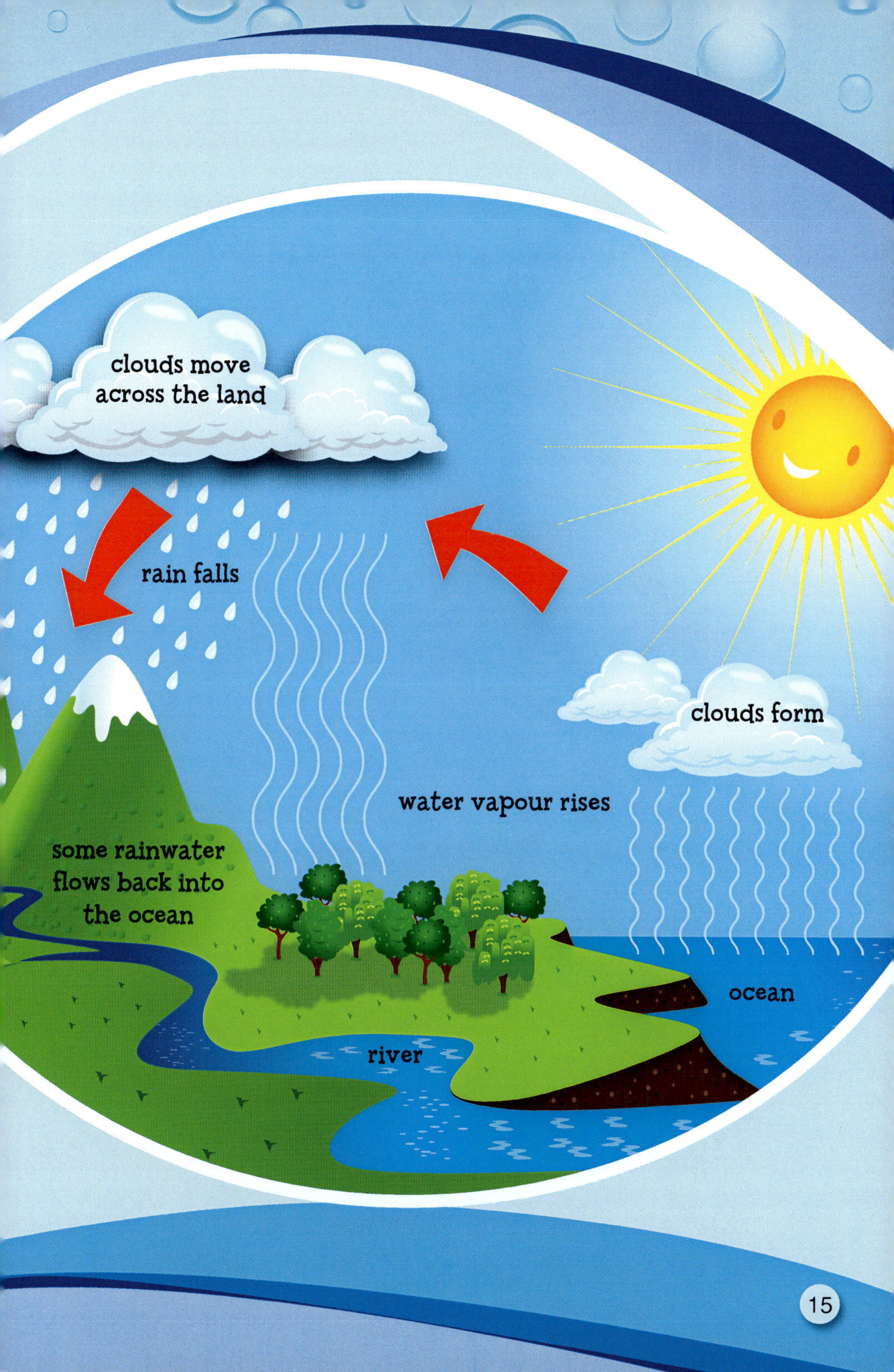
clouds move across the land
rain falls
clouds form
water vapour rises
some rainwater flows back into the ocean
ocean
river

So, do you want to know even more about the water cycle? Here are some interesting facts!

Fact 1

The water cycle is also known as the hydrologic cycle. Hydrologic (say: *hi-dro-loj-ik*) means "knowledge about water".

Fact 2

During the water cycle, water can be a **solid** (ice), a **liquid** (rain) or a **gas** (water vapour).

Fact 3

Along with rain, water falls to Earth as snow, hail or sleet. Sleet is snow that has started to melt.

Fact 4

The amount of water on Earth has stayed the same for around two billion years - wow!

Making Fresh Water

Did you know that salt water from the ocean can be made into drinking water? This process is called **desalination.**

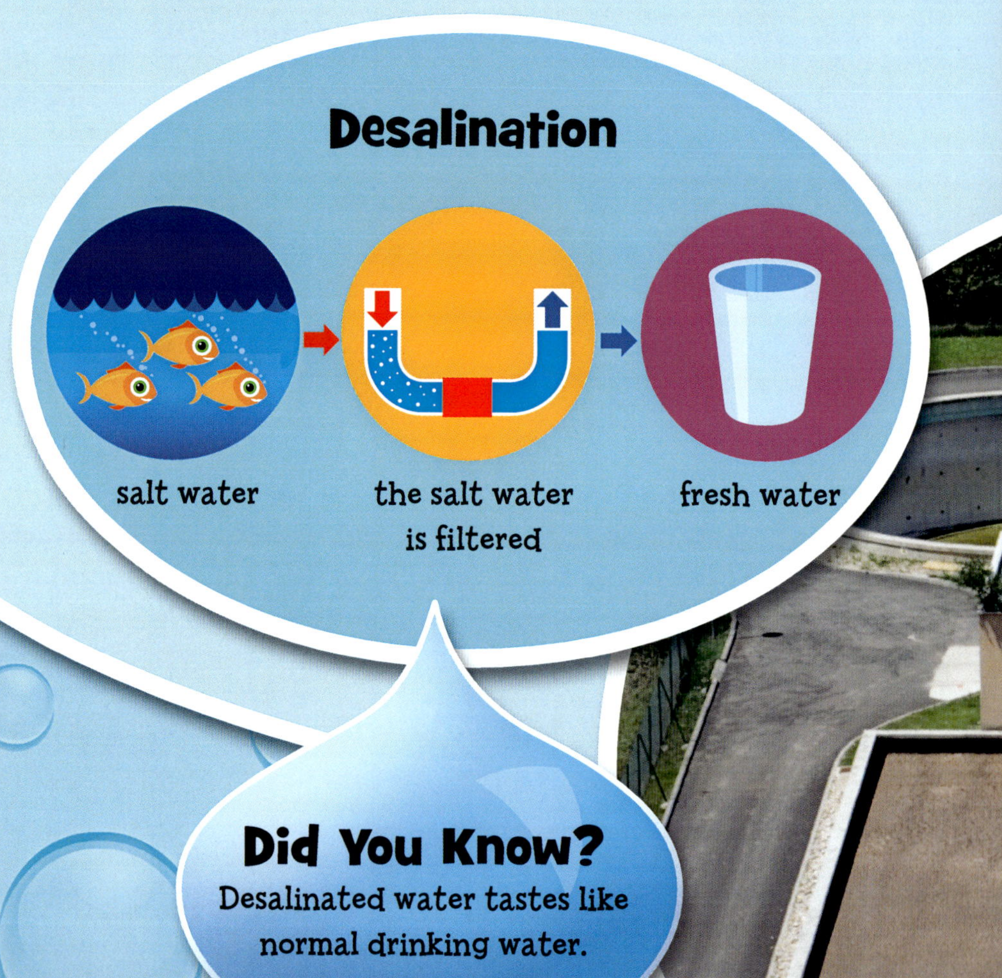

Did You Know?

Desalinated water tastes like normal drinking water.

Salt water is taken and pushed through filters at a desalination plant. The filters stop the salt and let the fresh water go through.

Does this mean we can use as much water as we like? No! Desalination uses a lot of **electricity**. The less electricity we use, the better!

There are thousands of desalination plants around the world.

Super Saving!

Now, you know that:

- All living things need water to survive.
- We use water in many different ways.
- There is only a small amount of fresh water on Earth.
- The water cycle is the journey water takes on Earth.
- We need to **save** water!

Everyone can be a super water saver. Here are some tips you can use at home.

Shower Power

Have a shower instead of a bath. Showers use much less water. Try to make sure your shower is three minutes or under. You can time yourself with an egg timer, or use an alarm clock.

Sneaky Leaks

Leaky taps are huge water wasters. If you find a leaky tap, tell an adult so they can get it fixed.

Use a Bucket

When you turn on the shower, it can take a while to warm up. This can waste a lot of water. Why don't you try collecting the water in a bucket? After your shower, you can use it to water the plants!

Turn It Off!

When you brush your teeth, don't leave the tap running – turn it off! You don't need any water until you're ready to rinse your mouth and toothbrush. This will save a lot of water!

Did You Know?

The bathroom is the room in the house where most water is used!

Think Before You Drink!

If you can, drink tap water instead of buying a bottle of water. Did you know that it takes around seven litres of water to make the plastic for just one bottle of water? Now that's something to think about!

Fill It Up

Don't turn on the dishwasher if it's half empty. Wait until the dishwasher is full of dirty dishes before you turn it on. You will wash more dishes and use less water!

Beat the Heat

The best time to water the garden is early in the morning or late in the afternoon. These are the times of day when the temperature drops. If you water when it's hot and sunny, the water will **evaporate** before the plants drink it. What a waste!

Who Needs a Hose?

Using a hose to wash your bike wastes a lot of water. Use a bucket and a sponge or cloth, instead. This will get your bike super clean and best of all, you will use less water!

Water Activity

Here is a fun water-saving activity that you can do at home.

What to do:

1. Draw a map of your home.
2. Circle all the places where water is used.
3. Visit each place. Think of ways to save water there.
4. Using your findings, write a water-saving plan for your home!

My Water-Saving Plan!

Problems	Solutions
Shower takes too long to warm up.	Put a bucket in the shower to collect the extra water.

Quiz

Are you a super water saver? Try this quiz to find out how much you know about saving water.

1. When is the best time of day to water your garden?

A Early morning or late afternoon

B At lunchtime

C All day long

2. Which of these things uses less water?

- **A** Having a shower
- **B** Having a bath
- **C** Having a bath while the shower is running

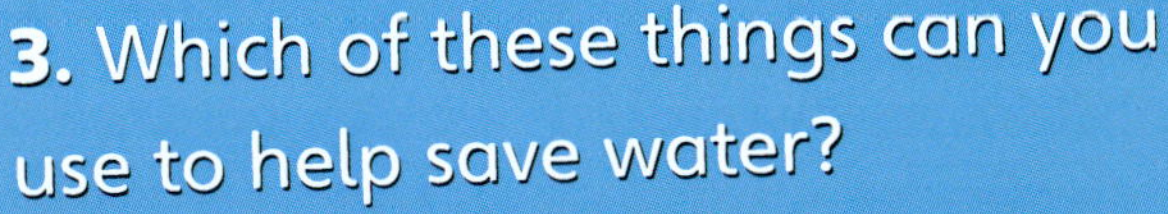

3. Which of these things can you use to help save water?

- **A** A bucket
- **B** An egg timer
- **C** Both

Quiz Answers:

1A 2A 3C

Glossary

desalination	taking salt out of seawater to make fresh water
electricity	a type of energy or power
evaporate	to change from a liquid into a gas or steam
gas	a substance that is like air; does not have a fixed shape
liquid	a substance that flows; does not have a fixed shape
process	a set of steps or events
reservoirs	man-made lakes used for storing water
solid	a substance that is firm; has a fixed shape
source	where something comes from
Southern Hemisphere	the bottom half of the Earth
survive	to remain alive
water vapour	water in the form of gas or steam